"Death and Life are in the power of the tongue…"

-The Book of Proverbs 18:21-

The Black Assassin:
Nigger Nigga Niggah Killaz

Between their births and their deaths,
Three out of ten are attached to life,
Three out of ten are attached to death,
Three out of ten are idly passing through.

Only one knows how to die and stay dead
And still go on living.

-The I Ching –

For All My Brothers Resting In Peace
(R.I.P.)

Home
Spirits whisper…
Take meeeeeeee…
Home
Land of Kings, Queens, Pharaohs, Warriors,
gods
I am coming
Pyramids, Sphinx, Ancestral Tombs
Take meeeeeeee …
Home
Bathe in the Nile
Desert sands between my toes
Smell the air atop Kilimanjaro
(Mountains on the moon)
Dance
To the rhythms of the Congo
I am coming…
Home

For the Lord says,
"In my Father's house, there are many
mansions"
"If it was not so, I would have told you"

"I go to prepare a place for you. So where I
AM you are there also"
Home…Heaven…Spirits…Whisper…
Mother
Afrika
My dear brothers
In God's time
I will join you
There…at the crossroads
In Heaven…
Home

We will dance the freedom dance
We will drink from the wells of joy
In the spirit of Afrika
The American nightmare will end
We will be home
We will all be together
Family
Eternity

Spirits…whisper…take ussssss
Home

TABLE OF CONTENTS

Part 1 Ninjitsu "The Art of Invisibility"

Nigger Nigga Niggah Killaz…   10
No Fair…………………………..   16
Hunting Season………………   17
Genocidal Suicide………..   19
American Roulette ……….   24
Black Supremacist…………….   26

Part 2 Bujutsu "The Dark Side"

Working for the Klan……   30
Loaded…………………..   41
The Living Dead …………….   44
Ghetto Poetry …………….   46
The "Nigga" that Tried to Kill the
President………………..   51
"The 3/5th Doctrine"
(The US Constitution)………….....   54

Part 3 Kindo "The Way of the Sword"

Rage …………………………   58
Strait Jacket ………………..   66

Nightfall (*The Deadly Game of Psychological Warfare*)....   68
How Long?   73
The Choice   75
Lil Half Dead   78

Part 4 Shariken and Tetsu-bishi "Razors and Spikes'

Black Assassin   82
Still A Slave...................   86
The "Nigga" Experiment......   90
To Live and Die in Black America   95
Aferica (*A New Movement*)...   101

*Hello America, welcome to the world of
"The Black Assassin"— I hope you brought
your hard hat...*

Here we go!

Part 1

Ninjitsu

"The Art of Invisibility"

Just do what needs to be done, and then stop.
Attain your purpose, but don't press your
advantage.
Be resolute, but don't boast.
Succeed, but don't crow.
Accomplish, but don't overpower.
                                    -The I Ching

NIGGER
      NIGGA
            NIGGAH
                KILLAZ

I watch you…
It's in the way you move
The way you talk
The way you stalk

The way you think
Your thoughts stink

I look into your eyes
Quickly
Before you look away
Dark eyes
Shark eyes
I listen to the words you say

I watch your lips
They reveal
The rottenness of your teeth
Your soul
You're a Nigger Nigga Niggah killa
Your spirit knows no peace
I observe

Your actions
If you talk the talk
Do you walk the walk?
Do you pay the cost?
False talk
False walk
We all pay the cost

You're a Nigger Nigga Niggah killa
But you "think" it's not your fault

Oh you're clever
Clever…like a snake
Nigger killer
Nigga Killa
Niggah killa
Never giving, always on the take

"Hey Nigger"
"Yo my Nigga"
"Them my Niggaz"
"That my Nigga"
"That Niggah there a fool"

 We all Niggers (so you think)
"We the 'new' Niggah"

"We the 'real true' Niggah"
"Nigga I'm gonna' kill that fake
              Nigga
                  Niggah.....Cool"

You spit out this vile poison
This so-called language of your inner-culture
Black people, let's be real
That ain't culture....It's more like torture

Spell it how you want
Say it how you want
You're a Nigger Nigga Niggah killa
But you don't get the point

It's not just what you say
It's what you **do**
Your action speaks louder than your word
So you "think" like a Nigger
So you "act" like a Nigga
So you "talk" like a Niggah
Because from birth till death;
Nigger/Nigga/Niggah is all you've heard

How does a Nigger think?
 ("Niggers ain't shit")

How does a Nigga act?
("Kill a Nigga")
How does a Niggah talk?
 ("Fuck you Niggah")

The same
No matter how you say or spell it
Nigger Nigga Niggah is still the name

Nigger killers
Nigga killaz
Niggah killaz
Nurtured by the White slave owners of the past
Niggers Niggaz Niggahz
Wake up! Wake up! Before you breathe your last

You shout out "Nigger!" "Nigga!!" " Niggah!!!"
Without ever "thinking", now that's the trick!
Wake up Niggers! Niggaz! Niggahz!
In this game you're getting your asses kicked

It's been beat into your sub-conscious
It's been whipped into your soul
Kill Nigger! Kill Nigga!! Kill Niggah!!!
"Nigga, don't question. Do as you're told

Cut a Nigger's throat
Blow a Nigga'z brains out

Use you machete, your 9mm, your uzi
"Don't think, Niggah! Do it! Don't doubt!"

So just like the house Niggers of old

You "new" Niggaz –
Niggahz do the job

Nigger dead
Nigga dead
Niggah dead
The white man's in your head;
he's your god
God of Black death
God of Black destruction
Nigger kills Nigga kills Niggah
Following the White man's instruction

This cultural schizophrenia is killing us
Wake up! Niggers, Niggaz. This is no game!
Stop trying to fool yourselves
Nigger, Nigga, Niggah is not your name!

When you "think' of yourself that way
You will "think" that way of us all
So when the White man's conditioning kicks
in…
Niggers
        Niggaz
                Niggahz….start to fall.

Hang a Nigger; Tar and Feather a Nigger
Shoot a Nigga; cut a Nigga; beat and stomp a
Nigga;Kill a Niggah; Break a Niggah'z back
Niggers unemployed on welfare
Niggaz doing crime; Niggas in jail
Niggahz selling drugs; Niggahz on crack

So I watch you…
I tell you you're the White man's "new" slave
As you tell your "homie" ,
"You're my main
                "Niggaz"
                        "Niggahz"

I tell you you're playing the deadly game of
death through deception
Your response, "How the fuck you figga?"
        (What a dumb ass Nigga)

You're slick
You're smooth
You're stupid
You're fools
You're a Nigger
                Nigga
                    Niggah killa
And you "think" that this is cool
        (You stupid ass Niggah)

So you continue this madness
You continue to poison our race
Wake up! "Brothers" and "Sisters"
Our culture is catching a 187 case

Every time you "think" or say Nigger, Nigga
Another "sister" and "brother" dies
Get that White man's bullshit out of your mind!
Stop believing his "true lies"

You say that you have taken the power over
this word
Flipped it and made it your own
But you can't stop, won't stop, can you "Nigga"?
Until all "Niggaz" are gone

You Nigger killers
You Nigga destroyers
You Niggah pawns for the White man
One day you're going to have to face the
looking glass
And then…

"Blow your fuckin' brains out…

   Nigger
     Nigga
       Niggah"

  "Quick! Right now!! Don't think!!
Do it fast!!!!"
Bang!
   Nigger
     Nigga
       Niggahz…you're dead

To stop acting like one
Stop thinking like one
If you want to kill one
Kill the one in your mind
Michael

NO FAIR

Welfare
Because you care
For my welfare
Don't you dare

Food stamps
More like, concentration camps
Where are the off ramps…
For me?

I want workdays
To earn my pay days
I don't want to just lay dazed
I want a job!

Welfare
Because you care
About my welfare
Bullshit!

Jail cell…
I'm in hell
Can't leave…
Can't breathe

Like I'm in a Gas chamber…
My life's in danger

This "system's "trying to
exterminate me

Welfare
Because you care
About my welfare
Bullshit!

HUNTING SEASON

Pants all sagging
Feet all dragging
Pony tail wearing
I' m a killer uncaring

Prowling the streets in search of blood
"What's up Blood?" "What's up Cuzz?"
I'm like a rabid dog unleashed
The human in me has died; only lives the beast

I'm a walking train wreck
With gold around my neck
Braids in my head
I'm the walking dead

Cruising the 'hood from seven to seven
Packing my shot gun, my "Nine" and my A-K 47
My drive-by leaves three shot to pieces
Crack selling. Hate swelling. The madness
never ceases

Proudly sporting my colors
Disrespecting my father and mother
For my 'hood, I'll even kill my own brother
I'm a psychopath undercover

Robbing your home for a couple of bucks
Raping your woman, not giving a fuck
Disrespecting my heritage, and saying, "So,
what's up?"
Destroying my culture, and saying, "Tough luck"

Creeping in the night
I'm like a vampire poised to strike
Looking for a fight
Looking to turn off your fuckin' lights

I'm a Black boy and I hunt Black boys
I earn my stripes by killing my own
"Black on Black "crime is real to me
It's "kill or be killed" …How is that wrong?

Figga' that shit out…'Cause I can't

"GENOCIDAL SUICIDE"

AFRICA AFRICAN AFRO
BLACK NEGRO COLORED
AMERICANS

CHOOSE YOUR POISON

Genocide; the systematic extermination of a
particular ethnic group
Suicide; knowingly and deliberately taking
your own life
If we don't react quickly this point will be moot
Or do you enjoy being used as laboratory mice?

I hear you bitching about the system
Making the White man your scapegoat
Just stop! Shut up!! Listen!!!
This could be your final hope

Racism may be institutionalized
But the mental slavery is self-imposed
You don't need riches to act civilized
You don't need government to save your soul

You will kill another brother and blame it

On the White man
You will sell your baby for crack
You will steal from your mother
And say," She just don't understand…"
Society has made you act like that

When you look at your heritage
You'll find it's not as honorable
as you'd like to believe
We participated in the enslavement of our people.

This was human sacrilege
Maybe this is the genesis of our disease

Some sold our people for the proverbial 30
pieces of silver

Opened the door for the mother country
to be raped
By our own hands the blood flows like a river
And we have the audacity to blame others
for our fate?

The "chains" you now display so proudly
about your neck

Represents the "slave collars"
worn by your ancestral sisters and brothers
If you think you can't do more than get a
welfare check
You disrespect the blood, sweat and tears of
your hard working grandfathers and mothers

That nice "whip" you drive, the diamond rings
You got from selling out the Blacks
That new home of your dreams
It's you who now put the "whip" to our backs

Wearing your designer clothes and six
hundred dollar shoes
As you turn your face to those in the streets
"More mass murdering in the inner city"
Reports the nine o'clock news
And our tomorrows look like an instant repeat

Now keep pretending that you don't know
Continue to close your eyes to the truth
Soon, very soon, you shall meet your true foe
Staring back from the mirror, that enemy is you!

STOP! SHUT UP!! LISTEN!!!

To a story of mankind
The story of brothers named Abel and Cain
When a brother murdered his brother
Thus committing the shame above all other shame

As the story goes,
Ham's lineage was cursed as a race
But any curse can be broken
In the presence of God, they pleaded their case
So by grace a new day has awoken

That's why I just don't understand,
The hate I see, when you look at me
The fire in your eyes, tells me you want me to die
The snarl on your face, tells me you hate your race
The malice in your voice,
says you're a self-destructive force
Your body language,
spells beware of danger

You want to kill me, don't ya'?
So there will be more "leftover" for you
More what?

When will you take your status serious?

You've already gone to red alert
Stop exclaiming, "He's paranoid, he's delirious"
Stop exacerbating your pain.
Stop perpetuating your hurt
Choose your poison
Genocide or suicide

The results will be the same

Death wish
We're now infamous for inventing a new term
To my knowledge "genocidal suicide" has
never been done
Today we face a double whammy,
but it's not too late to learn
That we can become famous
for our ability to overcome

Massive cuts in educational grants and loans
Genocide
Killing and stealing and burning down our
homes
Suicide

Generations of welfare
and welfare and welfare

Genocide
Gang banging, dope-selling, street warfare
Suicide
Being mistreated due to the color of your skin
Genocide
Constantly degrading and
demeaning each other
Due to the condition we're in
That's suicide
A society that rewards our women
for the Black man not living in the home
Genocide
Leaving our women and children uncared for
and all alone
Suicide
Overturning affirmative action
and civil rights gains
Genocide
Selling your food stamps for crack to help
buffer your pain
Suicide
Overturning pro-choice
and disrespecting the equal rights amendment
Genocide
Refute of "The Word of God"
and disobeying its commandments

Suicide
Giving tax breaks to the rich while taking
more from the poor
Genocide
Bleaching your skin, calling your woman
Bitch and Whore
Suicide
Cutting funding for youth
and the health care program
Genocide
Spending your money
with everybody but the black man
Suicide

STOP! SHUT UP!! LISTEN!!!

James Baldwin
THIS COULD BE OUR FINAL HOPE!

SIX-SHOOTER
AMERICAN ROULETTE
(From a Black Man's Perspective)

Click…

That's a sound I will never forget
Because every time I have unprotected sex
I play American Roulette

Click…

I must beware of AIDS
I'm in a high-risk group

Click…

"Black on Black" crime
I'm living on borrowed time

Education lacks
Welfare cutbacks

Click…

So hard to get a decent job

My family and I live like scavengers
One meal away before I starve
Disease and pestilence
are my death harbingers

Click…

I begin to sweat
I have no empty chambers left
One last chance is all I'll get
The next click means my certain death

But wait! A light goes on
I know what I have to do
The next click, a bullet to your fuckin' dome
Because when I play, you play too

I play American Roulette…
Because it seems like I have no damn choice

BLACK SUPREMACIST

You hate "all" White people
The bad and the good
You're a Black Supremacist
Still living in segregated neighborhoods

But the neighborhood of which I speak
Is all in your head
You refuse to see the truth
Your brain is dead

You believe in that bullshit philosophy of
" Black Supremacy"
That proclaims Black dominate
and White regressive genes
"Black Supremacy" is just as ridiculous as
"White Supremacy"
They're both on the same losing team

You talk about the melanin in your skin
You say that's proof that you are "superior"
That's the same racist doctrine as
"White Supremacy"
In order to be "superior" it has to make
          someone else "inferior"

You like to proclaim that black man
racist ass ideology
You call it "Africana Study" or "Pan
Africanism"
You teach Blacks that they ruled the world
But you don't teach about Black on Black
barbarism and cannibalism

So before you start screaming,
"Blacks can't be Racist, or Supremacist!"
I want you to think about this,
Remember when you ran around screaming
"Black Power!"
And doing it with a black glove on your black
raised fist!

Remember when you looked down on some
White people
You called them "poor white trash"
Because now you have a Ph.D. by your name
And you're making a little cash

Remember when you got angry
with that Black woman
Because she choose to be with a White man
You think your dick is bigger than his

But it takes more than a big dick
to make you a man

You think HBCs (Historical Black Colleges)
should be "FOR BLACKS ONLY"
How soon you forget the signs that said,
 "FOR WHITES ONLY"

Yeah you're a "Black Supremacist",
but to me you're just a fuckin' phony

Part 2

Bujutsu

"The Dark Side"

Which is more precious, fame or health?
Which is more valuable, health or wealth?
Which is more harmful, winning or losing?

Knowing what is enough is freedom.
Knowing when to stop is safety.
Practice these, and you will endure.

-The I Ching -

WORKING FOR THE KLAN

You thought that you were slick
You didn't think anyone would know
That you're an undercover trick
And your cover I'm about to blow

You work for the Klan
And you're a Black man
With a Black sheet
Covering your White mind
You work for the Klan
By killing off your own kind

I think you got "punk" in you
Because you're afraid
To stand up and say, "I refuse!"
"To choose, to kill another brother"
Leaving his mother
Suffocating in her pain
But you have no shame

You say,

"Fuck you punk
I gotta' eat

Dogs eat dog
That's the code of the streets"

"I'll steal,
And kill
I'll slang
And bang
I'll rape
And take
To put food on my plate"

You say,

"I don't want to hear
That we're "sisters" and "brothers" shit
You weak ass bitch
So fuck you again
You little fag
And if I catch you around here again
I'll put my foot in your punk ass"

I say,

"You fool!
You idiot!!
What kind of Black man is he?

Using this tired lame ass excuse
To kill off a good "brother" like me"

You say, "Hustle or starve"
How about, "Go get a fuckin' job"

If you really were that hard
I'll tell you what you would do
You would stop working for the Klan
And you would start working for you
Because when you work for yourself
You work for all of us
Our life means the Klan's death
"Brothers," get off the back of that mental bus

Now if you continue to work for the Klan
I'll tell you where our culture will go
On a one-way ticket to genocide
"But you don't hear me though"

PART II

You work for the Klan
And you call yourself a "Patriotic American"
You call yourself a White person with an
"open mind"

Subtlety killing off others who aren't your kind
You're the first one to say
"No, not me, I have many Black friends"
You're taking the express lane to hell
Hypocrisy is your sin

You ask, "What do you mean?"
"Could you please explain yourself?"
It's called accessory to sin
And the sentence is eternal death

When you hear a racist joke
And you act like you didn't
When you give others that "look"
And pollute the books you've written

When you let "the system" work for you
You know that "Good Ole Boy" Network
And scream "Reverse Discrimination!" To
Affirmative Action
Boy, you really know how to dish out the dirt

When you let the violent actions of the Klan
Become your silent voice
Your silence becomes an admission of guilt
Their choice becomes your choice

When you say "Black people are cool with me,
But I wouldn't want one to date my sister"
You're feeding into that Klan mentality
Because most of us don't want your sister,
Mister

PART III

You thought that you were getting away
You thought that no one would see
That you're an undercover snake
And your soul can be bought for a fee

You call yourself a real "Nigga"
And you spell it with a"g-a"
You don't fool me. You work for the Klan
The hell with what you say
You sell the "brothers" and "sisters" dope
You call it slanging cane
You say, "If I don't do it, somebody else will"
"So it really ain't no thang"

You're out there banging, stealing, robbing
You'll kill another "Nigga"
that ain't from yo' hood

I can hear the Grand Wizard of the Klan
saying,"You "Niggaz" with the "g-a,"
are doing real good"

And what you do next
Is worst than anything you've ever done before
You blame the "White Man"
You say he won't let you get your foot in the door
But when I ask, "When did you try" …you lie
And say, "What the hell you wanna' know for"

And you have the nerve to quote Malcolm X,
with your lazy "triflin" ass
I try to tell you Malcolm preached "self-help",
You say, "Don't make me laugh"

So you keep on….

Killing and stealing
Instead of living and building
You will rob
Instead of getting a job
Be a fool
Before you go to school
Destroy your community
Instead of promoting pride and unity

The Crips, The Bloods,
They work for the Klan
The Latin Kings, The El Rookins
They work for the Klan
"MS13" and "18 Street"
I guess "666"
Ain't the only number of "The Beast"
The Gangsta' Disciples and the Vice Lords
They work for the Klan
Killaz of young Black and Brown Boys

Yeah, you work for the Klan
That's your full-time job
There must be a hole in your head
Because ignorance is your god

PART IV

I hear you rappers rapping about the streets
You say, "I gotta' stay true to the game"
You talk about the "bitches" and "ho's" you meet
"After all," you say, "What's in a name?"

So now young White, Asian, and Latino youth
Are calling themselves" Niggaz" too;
They say that's how they "stay true"
Because you make them think it's "cool" to
be a "Nigga". I say," Who's playing who?"

They won't call themselves "Crackers",
"Slant Eyes", or "Beaners"
And I bet neither will you
Because unlike you they know the truth
That disrespecting your ancestors
doesn't make you "cool"
It makes you a fucking fool
(Now that's really what they think of you)

I give you credit, you got these White and
Asian parents shitting their "dirty draw's"
Because their cute "little pimply face boys"
are showing their ass and holding their balls

Instead of "Leave it to Beaver";
they now got "Jungle Fever"

From Asia to Europe, this is your contribution
Hatin' your own kind. Defies nature's laws
That's why some people still think we Blacks
have tails; you further the Klan's cause

So you let Eminem busta' ass and others,
into your "Nigga fold"
And just like their ancestors of old,
they're gonna' take all the gold

I know the game so I told the game….
You sold the game and he stole the game

Young money is dumb money

And before long, you'll all be working for him,
cleaning and polishing his 24inch "rims"

Instead of calling him Eminem,
he'll have you calling him "Massa M"

Russell Simmons'/Def Comedy
(Buck Yo' Eyes) Jam
Gets him his Klan membership card
They're his "Fam'"

Jay Z and Kanye West,
("Illuminati", not hardly)
They work for the Klan's Lynch Party

Even with all that cash,
they don't get a pass…

"Too Live Crew";
Exploiters of young Black girls' honey
All Klan members…
Bought with "Blood Money"

So you continue to say "Fuck this, fuck that"
"Motherfuckaz, punks, and bitches"
"Shit, ass, tricks, fags, pussies,
ho's and snitches"
As our people grow poorer in spirit;
you continue to count your riches

Yeah, you're working for the Klan
As you shout out "Freedom of Speech!"
You're a true American now
Wearing your red, white, and blue sheets

PART V

Just a quick word for you dudes in school
Always acting a damn fool
You obviously work for the Klan
"Cause you think being disruptive in class is cool

There's always a few of you
Whose Klan job is to keep the other
from getting that knowledge
You want to keep your Homies ignorant and dumb
To get them into a prison cell…
instead of into a college

It's easy to spot you out…
Guess who disrupts the class?
Every time teachers try to teach;
why is it always your stupid ass?
Yeah the Klan trained you well,
but I wont give your dumb ass a pass

And most of you are young Black boys
Now how crazy is that shit
You do the dirty work of the Klan
 but you're too stupid to even know it

Now if you want to stop working for the Klan
Then I'll give you this last chance
When you go to class tomorrow
Let some other fool in school do the
White man's "buck dance"

But you can't...can you?

PART VI

You, yeah you... You work for the Klan too
Because they call you Hick or White Trash
You blame us Blacks for taking your jobs

Like we're just breaking our backs to make
that little cash

So you call us Nigger and Coon
Spade and Porch Monkey
And we call you Cracker and Red Neck
Pecker and White Honky

Due to our horrible conditions
We blame each other
You would like to hang my Black ass by a rope
While I would like to blow your brains out
You White motherfucka'

Because of what your "others" have
You think you should be better than me
You need someone to look down upon
Your anger won't let you see

You only see their fine cars and clothes
Their expensive jewelry and luxurious homes
Your skin is the same as theirs…?
But you sit in a sewer, while they sit on a throne

So you need someone else
of which to blame your fate

So you start working for the Klan
and you learn how to hate
But when you work for the Klan,
there's a trick
Because they'll cut your fuckin' throat
if you try to switch

PART VII

You thought that you would slither by
You're as poisonous as a scorpion's sting
You're a liar, a conniver, a black widow in hiding
When it comes to deception; you are the King

You work for the Klan
Because you "think" that you have "overcome"
You're living the "American Dream" now
How could a smart Black man like you
be so damn dumb?

You have a nice car and a nice home
You can get the job of your choosing
Yeah, you live in white suburbia now
While where you came from is steadily losing

The strength that you have now

You got it from "The Hood"
But since you've been working for the Klan
You don't give back, where it does the most good

You have intelligence, a positive attitude
You "had" sensitivity to your people's plight
But now you're a "Sambo", a "Tom" a "Sell-out!"
Living Black by day, living White by night

Yeah, you work for the Klan because you
believed the hype. You thought it was true
Until they broke into your house in suburbia
and beat that Black ass
Until it turned red, white and true blue

Don't you try to come back to the 'hood
We don't need any more traitors in our midst
You should have remembered where you
came from; fool
Because now you're on the brothers' "hit list"

PART VIII

And now you; yeah you, you work for the Klan
And I'll tell you why I saved you for last
You do more damage than all the rest

You control our present, future and past

You write the laws, you interpret the laws
You vote for and veto the bills
You make these racist's doctrines legal
Yeah you make it legal to be racist
and legal to kill

Just by your mannerisms,
your attitude and gestures
A nation of "wanna-be" racists
will follow your lead
And up pops the swastikas and combat boots
It's you who promote that "Klan mentality"
It's you who plant the seed

So when they beat a motorist in Los Angeles
I say, "Remember Rodney King"
"Stand Your Ground Law"
Trayvon Martin…I can still hear his last screams

Three Strikes Initiative;
Millions of Black and Brown Boys in prison
Reversal of Affirmative Action;
More Black Boys in jail than the College system

Yeah, all of you work for the Klan
He's your "Main Man"
Your mind, body, and soul is his
Whatever you do next
Don't claim that you didn't know
Because, "It is what it is"
"But you won't hear me though"

LOADED

I'm hot
Burning hot
I always seem combustible
Like a spark
Pleading to be ignited
I'm hot
Nuclear fission hot
I just can't seem to fight it

My blood is boiling
Steaming…piping hot
There seems to be no release for this heat
Soon…I'm going to explode
I'm the Tornado's eye
I'm loaded
Somebody's going to die

I hear my heartbeat
Sounds like the thunder of earthquakes
My nerves stand on edge
Pins and needles
Egg shells
My sanity is unwrapping
Like a hurricane

I have to happen

My thoughts have mutated
Xenophobic
Sentient
Hybrid being
I must survive
"By any means necessary"
I'm hot… I'm loaded
My humanity is first to die

All are my prey
No color lines here
My eyes shift
Left…right…left…right
I hunger
The heat intensifies
I'm hot
Somebody's mother cries

I'm dangerous…
Simmering
Far beyond the boiling point
Blazing heat
Suffocating
I must find a release

Targets…everyone's a target
More young souls…Rest In Peace (R.I.P.)

O-o-hhh ….
I'm so hot
And I'm fully loaded
Aimed Detonated
Ignited…Lit...exploded!!

A-a-hhh…
Its hell fire
Burning up my soul
Desperate to get out
Needing…pleading to get out
So hot…at any second I'm going to explode!

O-o-hhh…..Help…
…Don't help . .me...
….Help .. don't . ..help…
        A-a-hhh … it burns so good

O-o-hhh … A-a-hhh …
        …The heat … is volcanic
                …tremendous …
        …pleasurable …
                …pain …Has become my lover

…burn …
… baby …
… burn …

You busters better run for cover

THE LIVING DEAD

Hair uncombed
Beard growing too long
Filthy ragged clothes
With snot running from my nose

I'm a grown up man with beaten red eyes
Crying, "Can you spare a dime?"
I have no pride

Liquor store to liquor store
Street corner to street corner
"We don't want you around here anymore"
Begging for hand-outs
Society says get out!

Windshield wiping
To keep my crack smoke piping
Gas pumping
Saying, "I gotta' do something"

Run down
Out of bounds
No ground
To stand

A beat back
No slack
Off track
Anti-man

Shopping cart toting
Cigarette butt smoking
Aluminum tin can collecting
Garbage can inspecting

I am the father of our present
What an unholy nightmare
Where is the father of my past (my Dad)?
That bastard, never really cared

To allow his son to become such a wreck
Now you know why I can't put my own
fuckin' son in check

GHETTO POETRY

They call me Mr. D and this is what I see…..

A baby cries, he/she has no milk
Little boys play football on concrete streets
"Got to get home before I get whipped"
First rule of the ghetto is paranoia,
trust no one you meet

Young men congregate on street corners
to form gangs
While older men hide their faces in the shadows
They cringe from the light
because it reveals their pain
As they fight unemployment and peer
pressure, a losing battle

Young women experience pro-creation
from the back seat of a car
Young men learn responsibility
from fathers who ran away
Most of their children don't know
who their fathers are
Most of the mothers only wanted
an increase in welfare pay

A mother sells her food stamps,
she would rather have crack
An old lady goes to meet God,
from the blows of a baseball bat

Junkies in the streets, anxious to find a vein
AIDS festers here
Using dirty needles again and again
Death, they don't fear

Preachers spreading God's Word
Sunday morning
Prostitutes spreading their legs Sunday night
Pastor drives a Cadillac
with the congregations' earnings
Taken from grandmothers/grandfathers
that never learned to read or write

Thieves at the back door,
bill collectors at the front
Black man wants my women/
White man wants my vote
I make no excuses for being so blunt
You grew up here too, how'd you cope?

A twelve year old boy,
tugs at my coat
He doesn't want candy
He wants to sell me some dope

Pimps pimping
Pushers pushing
Hookers hooking
Bookies booking

Playing the lottery every day of your life
Hoping and praying for your number to come up
It's God who has numbered your days and nights
Even if you do win, be careful,
you might get stuck up

Family feuds
Unemployment blues
Poor people stealing
Old people ailing
The government's killing…
All of us

Middle class, upper class Blacks
Have turned their backs
They've fallen victim to the,

"I got mines, you get yours disease"
Pull yourself up by your own bootstraps

So they move away
Pretend not to hear what their people say …
    "Help me, help us, please"

Gun carrying thugs/out to spill blood
Law abiding citizens are their prey
Soon we'll all be like Clint Eastwood,
"Go ahead punk, make my day"

A welfare mother drives a brand new Cadillac
A blue-collar laborer has to pay back tax
All is fair in love and war
In the ghetto, all is fair in survival, Jack

Here's more…

Men finding escapism in a bottle
Ripple, Jim Beam, Jack Daniels
Have become their best friends
"A Nigga' ain't shit," has become their motto
It doesn't take a prophet
to figure out how this will end

Some of us would rather switch than fight
As a con-man plays his symphony of deceit
A man can't be beaten if he holds on tight
To his integrity and spiritual beliefs

A liquor store and a church on every block
The Lord giveth and the Lord taketh away
We secure our homes with bars and pad locks
We live in jungles even in these modern days

The homeless roam the streets,
as Slum Lords get rich
Single parent homes,
ghetto life's the pits

Both parents working nine to five
Latchkey kids left all alone
The 80s, 90s and 2000s will be remembered
As the decades the family died
and the children were neglected
With no place to call home

"Big Brother's" painting a masterpiece of
genocidal destruction…

Sirens screaming
People pipe-dreaming
Cat's cater-wauling
Profane name-calling
Dogs in heat
The smell of dead meat
Car tires burning rubber
Angry shouts from a mother
Airplanes booming
Motorcycles zooming
Buses, trucks, cars, trains,
Fussing, fighting, blazing sun,
pouring rain
Helicopters whirling
        Jheri curling
Horns blare
We change the color of our hair
Fake contact lenses
Hair extensions
Bleaching our skin
Hypocrisy is our sin
Ghetto boxes blasting
Ignorance everlasting
Building to a cacophony of madness

Bang!
Halt! Before I shoot! (Again.)
Spread 'em boy! You know the routine!
A worried mother greets
an unexpected phone call
With a bone-chilling scream

Children learn to speak English courtesy
          Of their favorite rap groups
Most believe their only way out is through
Music, crime, selling drugs,
or shooting the hoop

We give up our birth name
for street names
When we should give up our street names
for Afrikan names
Growing up "in the Ghetto" is not a shame
But, it's a damn shame
if you let the Ghetto grow in you

Even in madness, there is rhythm

THE "NIGGA" THAT TRIED TO KILL THE PRESIDENT
(President Barrack Obama, that is)

Every time President Barrack Obama opened
his mouth
This old "nigga" hated his every word
Ideas that he himself had once embraced
Now sounded foolish and absurd

And when President Obama grinned,
That really pissed this old "nigga" off
That's when this "nigga' decided he would
kill the President
No matter what the cost

But this old "nigga" wasn't stupid
He had played the game for a very long time
So he would lie back like a Stealth Bomber
Before he could pull off the perfect crime

"Yes Mr. President, we want to work with you"
This old "nigga" lied through his teeth
But in his heart he had just one mission
"This President I must defeat!"

So this old "nigga" plotted day and night
And convinced other "niggaz" to join him
(they were ready to go)
And every time the President would say
"Yes we can"
He and his "niggaz" would "just say no"

But the President wasn't a punk.
He met their dare with a dare
"If you won't work with me,
then the American people will", he declared
Now millions more Americans have
healthcare, they even call it "Obama Care"

Now this made this old "nigga"
as hot as fuckin' fish grease
I think he may have even "pissed" his pants
Because the people started screaming
"Yes we can! Yes we can!"
While he and his "niggaz" were still saying,
"No we can't"

So now this old "nigga'z" calling on his
"Supreme Niggaz"
To overturn this healthcare law.
They say it's "unconstitutional"

It doesn't matter that the Presidents'
a constitutional scholar
Because these "niggaz' " "nigga-isms"
are completely institutional

So when the President started creating jobs
These punk ass "niggaz" said "Let Detroit fail!"
Just because they wanted to kill the President
They didn't give a damn about the people
who would catch even more hell

Then these "niggaz" did something so crazy
It had never been done in the history of the
American people
They refused to pay the American debt
To kill the President they were willing to kill
the American people

They don't want to give him credit
for saving Wall Street
And putting Main Street back to work
Or for killing Osama Bin Laden
and bringing our troops home from war
Before more were killed, maimed or hurt

These "niggaz" don't want to give

President Barrack Obama credit
For saving America from another depression
Or for restoring America to its greatness in
the eyes of the world
They just want to teach this President a lesson

So they call him names like arrogant,
conceited, aloof, professor
A socialist, communist, a dictator, a
separatist, even a racist
These "niggaz" have gone crazy!
You see everything was cool for 200 years,
when the Presidents had only white faces

But like I said this President ain't no punk
So he eats their lessons for lunch
And if he was a white boy,
these "niggaz" would have crowned him "King"
And by now would be kissing his pinky ring

Yeah I called you old ass white boys "niggaz"
I know you don't like it, so stop acting like one
You thought only "niggaz" could be "niggaz",
you "niggaz" are so dumb
Not knowing, it's not the word, but your
actions that makes you one

I bet you didn't see that coming

No I don't think that all White people are
racist…only the ones that are
And all White people ain't "niggaz",
but there are some that are

I guess I won't be getting invited to the
White House anytime soon…
What do you think?

"THE 3/5th DOCTRINE"
(The United States Constitution)

Now this shit I've never been
able to understand
What kind of mind decides another man
is 3/5th of a man?

Where the hell did that number come from?
Why not 4/5th or 2/5th or even one?

What kind of mind decides how much
of a man is another?
This gotta' be the mind
of a sick ass mothafucka'

What kind of mind
thinks of another man as a fraction?
What kind of mind
then justifies this action?

What kind of mind calculates
the worth of another human being?
And thinks it knows more
than the almighty "Supreme Being"?

What kind of mind
takes the time to contemplate shit like this?
It was the mind of the White man
that did this shit

And this disturbed mind
had the balls to put that shit in writin'
And declared a Civil WAR,
White man on White man fightin'

(Now you know that's some serious shit)

Yeah I know you think it was for money,
but even if that's true
It's still some crazy ass shit,
'cause that 3/5th of a man was you

Yeah I know you think t
hey don't do that shit no more
Wanna' bet? They now build prisons
based on your 3rd grade reading score

They "flipped" the 3/5th Doctrine
and put it into the schools
And our little Black boys help carry it out
by actin' a damn fool

If you can't read
then you can't think
If you can't think
you can't make good choices
You won't have the tools
to be successful in school
Making it easier for you
to give in to street forces

I know most of you don't believe this shit
'Cause you would have to change yo' ways
You would have to teach
yo' Lil' boy to behave
And the 3/5th Doctrine
would finally be dead in its grave

Fuck the 3/5th Doctrine…

Part 3

Kindo

"The Way of the Sword"

No tiger can claw him.
No buffalo can gore him.
No weapon can pierce him.
Why is this so?
Because he has died,
there isn't anymore
room for death in him.
-The I Ching

RAGE

Come…
Journey with me to a place where
insurmountable energy
Has been entrapped for countless years
Where emotions have been suffocated
Hope crushed. Love mutilated
Dreams turned into nightmares

Come with me,
To a place where darkness beats out the light
And spirits are left unsatisfied

Come…
Take this journey and begin to understand
The essence of **RAGE** …
the soul of a Black man

Let's begin, before birth
Where the spirits are being formed
Before God brings to this earth
His miracle to be born

Where all beginnings are the same
And the stars are the limits
Where evil has no claim
And we all are meek and timid

Creation gives to human-kind
A gift of immeasurable worth
Now begins the time
Of hell, right here on earth

I cried when I was born…
I should have been forewarned
My comely essence was torn apart
And thrown into the fires of confusion
I curse this world daily for its unwanted
intrusion

As an infant it was only a feeling
I was much too young to understand
That on earth, early starts the killing
Of the life of an American Black man

I know people suffer all over the world
And our spirits suffer together
But in a land that could be a perfect pearl
I feel cursed to suffer for triple forever

As a child I grew up poor
And believe me children do know
That poverty is more than a state mind,
It's a state of being
I had no place else to go

Watching the Brady Bunch,
Leave it to Beaver
And Father Knows Best,
Good Times, Sanford and Son
Easy for me to see, who has more
And who has less

Ghetto life . . . .
Dog eats dog and rat eats rat
Blacks prey on Blacks to survive off crumbs
No one wants to live like that

You still don't understand, do you?
Come, let us journey further ....

"Yes Massa, no Massa"
"Yes boss man, yes"
Say it with that Nigger grin on your face
You like being a slave, don't you boy?
"Yes Massa, yes"

Hey you! You Black winch
Come share my bed
Please your Massa, you little bitch
But first take a bath and comb your nappy head

Hey boy, pick that cotton

Bail that hay
If you're really good, you may kiss my White ass
Free of pay

Your kids are filthy animals
My god says you have no soul
You're savages and beasts, no more than chattel
Now fetch my slippers and wipe that snot
from your runny nose

Can you feel it now?
No, not yet?
Let's continue on …

Educated by civil rights
As a teen I began to understand
Boycotts, sit-ins, riots, vicious fights
Proudly holding up my sign exclaiming …
"I am a man!"

I became addicted to a dream
And astonished by a man
His name was Dr. Martin Luther King
And he led a multitude of former slaves by
the hand

To equal rights, civil rights, human rights
The right to vote and be counted

I sometimes wake up in the dead of night
Wondering…
If you'd lived, how much more our people
would've amounted

Let us fight fire with fire!
We're sick and tired of this mess!
We shall take our respect!
"By any means necessary"
By any means we desire
Fight and kill and die for your manhood!
Says Brother Malcolm X

Martin wanted the ballot and got the bullet
Malcolm wanted the "bullet or the ballot"
They both got both
When our men stand up,
they're brutally shot down
My essence cries out,
I miss you both the most

As long as we scrub and wash, beg and plead
Shout Hallelujah! To God, praying on our knees
They say,
"Shut up! Be quiet. Leave truth alone"
"Forget Brothers Malcolm and Martin"
"The time of awareness is gone"

Burn… baby…burn

Let's continue …

WE ARE FREE!
Proud sons and daughters of Afrikan kings
My ancestors forged a nation
Proud sons and daughters of Afrikan queens
Never meant to slave on White man's
plantation

Afrikan soil beneath my feet
The smell of natural air
Free to hunt and kill what I need to eat
Free to venture where ever I dare

My names are Queen of Sheba
and Emperor Selassie

Not Boy, Nigger, Coon, Jungle Bunny or Spade
My heritage is so much richer and prouder
Than that which American has made

I arise with the sun, awakening with the Nile
I sleep with Egyptian pyramids and tombs
My intelligence molded the government you trial
My philosophers charted the stars and moons

I have vast riches and wealth
Jewels and gold adorn my temple
But my most precious crown is the value of self
What you think is complex, we make simple

Behold!
The only thing greater than thyself
The heavens are ours to praise
And you wonder why we prefer death
Rather than living here in American, as your slave

Can you feel it now?
A little
Good
Now I'm going to blow you away!

RAGE
It's killing babies for crack
It's heroin tracks

It's robbing and stealing and going to jail
It's infected by AIDS; it's living in hell
It's beating and lashing out at everything in sight
It has no knowledge of what's wrong or right

RAGE
It's being beat down and stomped on
Because of the color of your skin
It's being pounded and pounded
Again and again!!

RAGE
It explodes!!
It's more devastating than a nuclear bomb
Its residue lingers like radiation
Infecting our future fathers and sons

Listen
Stop playing with something
you can never understand
Set it free!
The spirit of the Black man

Or feel his wrath

You feel it now?   It's not over

The Rainbow Coalition, The NAACP
The Congressional Black Caucus

"The Black Church",
Nation of Islam's, "Honorable" Minister
Louis Farrakhan
Stop patting yourselves on the back
There's still work to be done!

Our sisters have turned their backs
on the brothers. This makes us mad
Our family structure has been shattered
Our Moms have become Dads

Our children are running wild in the streets
Their lifestyle molded by rap and BET

No heroes. No boundaries
No future hope
Sex is their religion
Violence is their Pope

RAGE
Manifests itself in all of these terrible forms:
Rape, child molestation, serial killings and porn

Feel it
It's growing
It could envelope a nation
For ***RAGE*** is contagious
Beware, you who blaspheme against God's creatio

RAGE
Because of you Sambo acting, assimilating
Pseudo Blacks
Because of the Klu-Klux-Klan,
White Knights
And their vicious racist attacks

RAGE
Because of innate institutionalized racism
And a White society with tunnel vision
Because of unequal treatment under the law
Corrupt government and unethical big business

RAGE
Because of a conscience permeated by evil
And hearts devoid of a soul
Because of a nation's unceasing greed
That de-values human life to the worship gold

RAGE
Because I have been
Colored, Negro, Black, Afro, African American
Treated like an un-welcomed guests
Because you have blamed me for me being here
If this is a life exam, you're failing the test

RAGE

Because you have freely opened the doors
For millions of others to prosper and grow
Them that now look down on me and laugh
As they pocket my money and turn up their nose

RAGE
Because you ridicule me for a language
I don't speak so well
Because your media constantly bombards me
subliminally. That I am destined to fail

RAGE
Because I am dying at a rate
far above the nation's average
Because you have taken my proud heritage,
And depict me as savage

RAGE
Because of defamation of character
and slanderous allegations
God will be your prosecutor
The devil's doing your litigation

RAGE
Because of punitive damages
Causing untold suffering and pain
I tell you love is the cure,
Nothing to lose, everything to gain

RAGE

Because of self-induced hate
That scars deep into my soul's core
Because it's God who decides my fate
And I won't take this bullshit anymore!

RAGE… what did you expect?

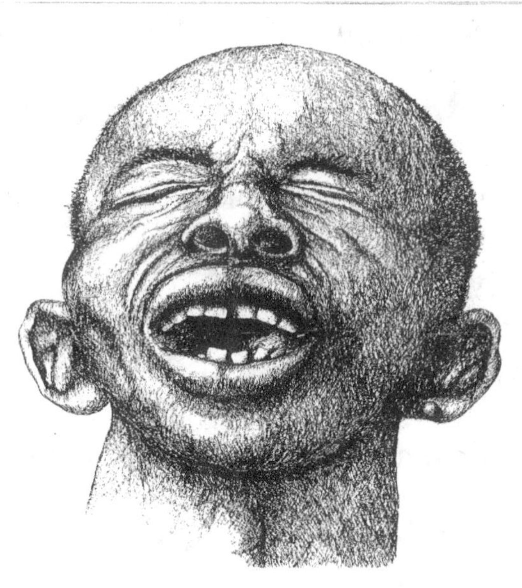

STRAIT JACKET

Because I am insane
My spirit is in unrest
Because I desire truth
Instead of being contented with lies
I am an outcast
Because I have gone beyond generalities
and stereotypes
The world has confined me in its rubber room
called society
I am utterly mad
For I wish to die
Instead of living in complete confusion

Purgatory
My mind has a will of its own
I am not rational
The world has driven me insane
I am put into a strait jacket woven in untruths

My emotions have been de-sensitized

Among billions
I am alone
For I cannot assimilate

into nonsense and frivolities
I analyzed the external
I found chaos
I searched inward
I found stability
In a world gone crazy
I am insane
Because I will not join in
My teachers/of limited knowledge
My employers/who control my livelihood
The preachers/of questionable faith
The lawyers/of man-made law
All conspire against me
My woman and children
Turn their backs on me
They say, "He's a dreamer"
For I choose solitude of self,
before family and friends
I choose the intangible spirit
instead of the tangible flesh
I choose the cool waters of self-restraint
instead of the smoldering fires of lust

I choose the self-education
of life's experience over
my college degree

Yet my teachers called me bright
I choose God over man
The preachers call me blasphemous
I choose peace of mind over my job
My employers say I don't follow protocol
I respect my own scales of judgment more
than the legal systems'
The lawyers want me jailed
It's true
I am insane …
I am as nutty as a fruit cake
I am one can short of a six-pack
Paddling up stream with only one paddle
All of my pistons are not firing
The world has driven me
unquestionably totally bananas
My arms have been tied
with straps of mal-content
Secured with locks of selfishness/envy/greed
Stashed away in a padded cell
Stuffed with
racism/sexism/materialism/hedonism
Trapped behind steel bars
molded with ignorance…

Waiting

NIGHTFALL
(The Deadly Game of Psychological Warfare)

The highest good is like water
which benefits all things
and contends with none.
It flows in low places that others disdain.
-Lao Tzu-

I am pain… Color me Black

Don't let anybody ever try to fool you
It all begins from within
Don't ever let them tell you
that it doesn't matter
It's always been more

than just the color of your skin

There is a place where evil dwells
And it poisons the souls of men
It confuses and perverts their minds
It makes enemies of would-be-friends

It uses fear and ignorance as it soldiers
Hate is its "Commander and Chief"
Survival is its pseudo-bait (red herring)
Death and destruction is its ultimate feat

So now you may enter my world
But, I must insist on telling you all
Come, enter this world of psychological warfare
Come, enter the world known as *NIGHTFALL*

THE HAMMER IS FALLING
The hammer is always falling
It can strike at any place, at any time

DEATH IS CALLING
Death is always calling
Tick tock…tick tock…listen to its chime
Silent sirens are blaring
These are the sirens of my mind

Awakening me to an unwanted consciousness
It's a reminder….it's "killing" time

Wake up; wake up….if you dare
See what I see
Everyone around me looks just like me
See what they want me to see
Everyone's acting the way they want us to be

Stop! Hush, be quiet….don't step out of line
Tick tock….tick tock….it's "killing" time

Off with his head
His heart
His nuts
We're the walking dead
Our future
No future
No us

I can't see who's doing this?
My foe seems invisible
I am being killed by words
Like "inalienable" and "indivisible"

I am walking with the dead

My "brothers' and "sisters" brains are gone
There are assassins in our ranks
So I am forced to walk alone

NIGHTFALL IS HERE
It's been here since the first yesterday
Nightfall is forever
Making free minds into slaves

THE HAMMER IS FALLING
The hammer is always falling
It may strike you next

DEATH IS CALLING
Death is always calling
American won't ever let you forget

Tick tock …tick tock…listen to its chimes
Tick tock…tick tock … it's "killing" time

The enemy is inside of me
It's inside of all of us
We are paranoid-schizophrenics
No one can we trust

You say, "Come … come with me"

"We can escape this way"
But I can see into your soul-less eyes
You're another assassin for pay
"Get back in line, you pseudo-human"
I am being whipped to death with a thought
"You're a savage beast, a Coon and a Nigger"
Locked in mental chains, waiting to be bought

"I wish you would, you mother fucker"
The hate in your eyes tell all
"Make a move and your Black ass is mine"
Beaten down to my knees, made to crawl

The glass ceiling
Intellect killing

And you thought you had gotten away

A 357 slug to the brain
Your bullet is your arrogance and pride
Out of your mouth spews fire and brimstone
Spreading half-truths and pious lies

THE HAMMER IS FALLING
The hammer is always falling
But it only seems to hit my kind?

DEATH IS CALLING
Death is always calling
In the nightfall of my mind

Tick tock … tick tock …
the clock is about to strike
Tick tock … tick tock …
and it only strikes at night

NIGHTFALL IS REAL
Although it doesn't touch, taste, or smell
In the game of psychological warfare
The mind tells the tale of living hell

FOUR WALLS CAVING IN
My soul's on the auction block
A strait- jacket imprisons my mind
And there is no key to this lock

Within this cell there are countless evils
Some so vile they have no names
When you force a mind to cave in on itself
Whatever happens next; who do you blame?

I sensed a great darkness covering the heavens
Its power came from spirits long oppressed

Harsh judgments were passed
on those it encountered
And only the pure of heart will pass its test

Those who had claimed the "light"
were consumed by the darkness
For they chose to "see" what wasn't there to see
NIGHTFALL covered the land called America
The home of the just, the brave, and the free

And with every judgment the darkness grew
Purifying itself, making itself stronger
Killing without sympathy or restraint
Until the "false light" would exist no longer

THE HAMMER IS FALLING
The hammer is always falling
But this time we have a new judge

DEATH IS CALLING
Death is always calling
Be it by fire, brimstone, or by flood

Tick tock … tick tock …
it's now a quarter of twelve
Tick tock … tick tock …

we're all going to hell

I am pain ---- Color me *NIGHTFALL*

TICK TOCK …
TICK TOCK …
TICK TOCK…

HOW LONG

Before you escape the mental slavery of the
Massa's whip
How long?
Before you stop using excuses for failing,
stop poking out your lips
How long?
Before you stop pointing your finger,
exclaiming,
"The White man's doing this. The White
man's doing that"
How long?
Before you stop talking about going back to
Afrika,
Realizing, where it is, is where you're at
How long?

Before you free yourself from this self-
destructive trance
How long?
Before you start playing the music, of which
you dance
How long?
Before you stop killing and stealing, stop
beating and cheating

Stop!
Doping your hope, stop hating your mate
Stop!
Moaning about your depressing state
Stop!
Crying and dying at a most alarming rate
Stop!
Bleeding and pleading for your
"true freedom" to come
Stop!
Screaming and dreaming when there's work
to be done

How long?
Before you start taking responsibility
for your children
Stop blaming others

Start honoring your father and mother,
respecting your sister and brother

How long?
Before you break free of the chains of the
"I couldn't", "I can't"
Stop!
Making excuses for not trying.
This is your chance
Stop!
Accepting living in conditions
fit for roaches and rats
Stop!
Fighting each other like dogs and cats

How long?
Before you stop giving your money to
everyone but yourself
Stop!
Living off welfare …
And find the true you within yourself

How long?
Before you Blacks who can help stop turning
your backs
Stop using that tired old philosophy

of "I got mines, now you get yours"
"Pull yourself up by your own boot straps"
Stop!
"Skinning and Grinning"
in the White man's face
Stop!
"Black on Black Crime"
catching a murder case
Stop!
Chasing and then erasing the
"American Dream"
Stop!
Faking and then taking
from the speeches of Dr. King
Stop!
Praying and then saying,
"Lord help me to hold out!"
Stop!
Teaching and then preaching
when you know you have doubt

STOP!!!

HOW LONG …

TIME'S UP!

THE CHOICE

Early morning let-downs
Mid-evening breakdowns
Midnight shake-downs

That's the blues

Babies crying, eggs frying,
My woman's crying
Because I'm still lying
On my lazy ass

Telephone's ringing
House needs cleaning,
But baby, I've been meaning
To look for a job

Dirty clothes,
My woman turns up her nose
I'm feeling real old
Where did my strength go?

Mixed matched shoes
Mixed matched socks
Trouble comes in twos

In this land of hard knocks

Broke my back
Stole my broken down Cadillac
They say I owe back tax
One drink away from a heart attack

A broken man,
I can barely stand
I need a helping hand
But there isn't any

With all my will
I still want to live
So I stumble out to give
All I have to give

My rent is due
Kids have the flu
What else can a man do?

That's the early morning blues

Bum a dollar to catch the bus
Scuffling and hustling from dawn to dust
From unemployment lines,

to welfare lines, to soup lines
No help here

Besides, a man's not a man
If he has to depend on welfare
Talking and walking, walking and talking
To myself

Reduced to begging and pleading
No chance of succeeding
This isn't living
It must be death

Boss say,
"No education, rise in inflation,
no sellable skill"
I may be forced to steal,
Or maybe to kill, just to pay my bills

No help wanted, no help needed,
no help in sight for me
But If I do a crime, I will do time,
can't make up my mind
Which way out do I choose?
That's the mid-evening blues

Didn't tell my wife, I took the knife
I may be forced to take a life to save my life
Don't have a plan, sweat on my hands,
I'm a desperate man

And I'm scared

Lurking and creeping, sneaking and peeping
In the dark like the other vermin of the night
Where is God?
He seems to have vanished from sight

A victim appears; a victim comes near,
a victim who fears
Victims are we both
Face to face
Our hearts both race
I cower in disgrace and make haste

Alone in my room, consumed by my gloom
Shaking and trembling
Because I've failed
For tomorrow shall come,
I'll have no place to run
Certainly this isn't heaven… Is it hell?

This is mid-night blues

This is all-night blues
This is the rest-of-my-life blues
For come tomorrow…
How then will I choose?

Knowing others is intelligence;
Knowing the self is enlightenment.
Conquering others is power;
Conquering the self is strength.

Lao Tzu-

LIL' HALF DEAD

At only eight years old
I was already sporting gold
Calling little girls bitches and ho's
Selling crack to buy my clothes
Failing in school. I say, "The teacher's a fool"
"I don't need to know no A,B,C's"
"Learn to read and write, Nigga' please"
I already got the "Nigga" disease

With cash money in my hand
I work for the dope man
My mom and dad, what a fuckin' joke
Begging me, their little boy, for a rock to smoke
Ditching class…Pants hanging off my ass
My homeboys taught me how to sag
They say "Fuck your mom and dad"
No one's ever home
I'm a latchkey kid left alone
Eight years old and already grown
Claiming a color in order to belong

No time for play time

Because the base heads are paying
Know what I'm saying?
Ice cream cone

Living in a danger zone
Playground…Battle ground
Sand box…Buck shots

The swings and slide
That's where my homeboy died
Playhouse…Madhouse
See saw…Fuck the law
Catch me if you can
This ain't no Disneyland

I never got a chance to get ahead…
So at only eight years old I was already
"Half-Dead"

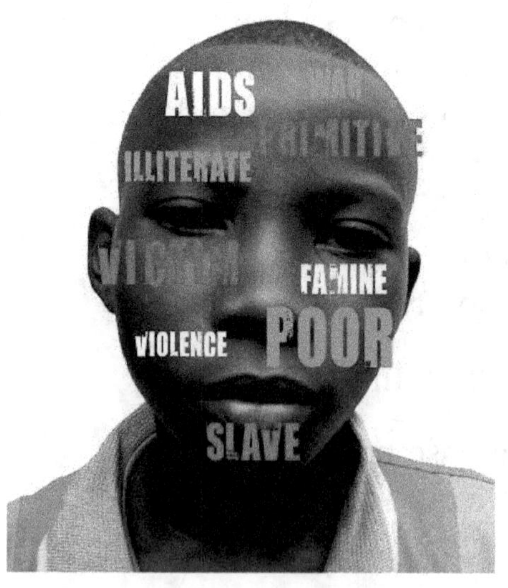

My words are very easy to understand,
very easy to put into practice. But you
"can't understand" them ,can't put them in
"practice. Words have their rule. Events
have their origins. People who can't
understand this can't understand me.
                              -The I Ching-

BLACK ASSASSIN

A man who tiptoes can't stand.
A man who straddles can't walk.
A man who shows off can't shine.
-Lao Tzu-

Greetings, I'm death/When I get through rapping, there won't be any of you punks left/Yeah I called you punks/ I eat yo' raps for lunch/Then shit them out 'cause they're wack/You fake Mack/The Black Assassin, that's me/I've come to destroy with this hard core beat/Raps made from kids, that's about

to change/Rappers with no meaning, I'll
hang/If you think I've come to make peace,
you're wrong/I came to declare War, go on/

I've come to kill ignorance and selling out/don't
run//You played yo'self "son"/You brag and
boast about being the best/About the "cake" you
bake/ and how well you dress/About how
"gangsta" you are, you gotta' be kidding/Don't
no gangsta sit on the toilet while he's pissing/A
gangsta wearing skinny jeans?/You're more like
a Drag Queen/Drama King/You say you got
"swag:/I say you got "fag"/ in you/in you
too/Yelling "Straight Out of Compton"/While
running "Straight Out of Compton/ You ain't no
NWA/ more like TWA/Talking all that shit about
how a Black man feels/Selling out wholesale, get
you for a steal/Yo raps are rejects/defects/ they
sell at the ninety nine cent store/I'm just getting
started/here's more/

Most of you are just boys, you've only begun
to live/So shut the fuck up and wipe the
dribble from your baby bib/ Assassinating
without discriminating/ Eliminating all
perpetrating/ Rapping like a two-edged
sword/I told you I was hard core/You remind

me of Sambo's sons/Talking bull-shit, you're so fuckin' dumb/A Black boy in white face/What a waste, what a disgrace/DJ Long Arms, Base

I've come, don't run/My lyrics are lightening, my voice is thunder/You say you've had enough, hmmm, I wonder?/Clown dancing and prancing/ hip-hopping and B-bopping/Draped in diamond platinum and designer sweats/Shouting phrases that are meaningless/Schools in session/ A history lesson/In Afrika the young brothers earned the gold they wore by giving to the tribe, not taking/ Stop faking/Pull your pants up and stop that ass shaking/fuckin' stripper nigga/before the brothers on the "Yard"/dicks start to get hard/That's where that sagging started/ Stop actin' retarded/Talking "bout how you rock the stage/More like, you're rocking AIDS/

The Black Assassin/Slaying losers/ and you who would use us/and abuse us/ and then accuse us/ of not "keeping it real"/You young clown/put that crack pipe down/I'm gonna' give you the ass whipping your daddy never

did/and put a lid/on your big ass mouth/no
doubt/No more selling out/ I know you
dudes/I looked you up on "YouTube A
Fool"/You young punks have been served/DJ
Long Arms, Word

I know I'm making enemies, did you think I
wanted to be your friend?/You help Black
boys kill Black boys and you call yourselves
Black men?/I know you want me to stop, but
I won't stop/ till you drop/You beg me,
"Please, no more"/Now who's the whore?/

You young girl rappers too/ Let me take time to
talk about you/I wouldn't dare call you women/
This ignorance has no limit/I'm not too timid/to
call you what you call yourself; BITCH/
Housewife of the "ATL" BITCH/
"The Queen BITCH"/"Stripper BITCH"/
"The get rich quick BITCH"/Basketball Wives
BITCH/Destroying little girls lives
BITCH/Getting' rich at any cost/
Turn that shit off/

You think this is cool/you fool/You're worst
than the dudes/You shake your tits and
wiggle your hips/you grind your ass and lick
your lips/I see you grab your pussy like you

were a dude/how rude/I even heard you call
your clit a dick/how sick/Rapping about what
good sex you have/ Don't make me laugh/we
dudes just one hit it and quit it/and laugh/ at
your stupid ass/"Young-Dumb-and- full- of-
cum"/ giving everybody some/

You say, "Bitch get paid for getting
laid"/That officially makes you a" Ho"/Now
you know/You got 12 year-old girls giving it
up/this is nuts/ you sluts/Are you going to
take care of this baby with a baby?/What if
she was your little sister?/ Would you dis
her?/ Jay Z, switched/and won't call you
BITCH/ "cause he birthed/on earth/ an
innocent little girl/into the world/ you
hypocrite/which is which?/I rest my case/
DJ Long Arms, Base

I bring the knowledge that send you poot
butts home/Call my lyrics the Malcolm X of
the microphone/They blaze like fire/ by any
means I desire/Yeah I called you a "poot
butt/"Google that shit up/I've come to kick
ass/ don't brag/You say I'm scary, that's my
job/'cause you ain't hard/I pulled your hold
card/That superficial bullshit you sing don't

mean a thing/I'm the "Godfather", kiss the pinky ring/

My concept is so fresh/You failed the test/It has its own style, I didn't smile/If you don't get it, you ain't wit it/Don't look at me strange, I'm not ashamed/To tell the world about your lame ass game/You're still in puberty waiting for your baby voice to change/I know why you punks need a body guard/'cause I was walking these streets before your little dicks started getting hard/

I'm here, you better fear/My words bring pain/ You ain't got game/You say, "The Black Assassin", who's he?/And what gives him the right to talk about me?/Another lesson, no more guessing, time for confessing/Start Texting/"The Black Assassin"/It's you, and you and you and you/you too/You who sell us out like Judas/You 're clueless/You're all saps with weak raps/Get the fuck outta' of my face/ DJ Long Arms, Base

I'm not finished, you wish/ Now comes the time I really start to dis/and dis-miss/You're just a child/ If you were mine you'd never be this wild/You older Black men you ought to be ashamed/Being led by punk ass kids with made-up street names/While our people are dying from within/I'm eliminating all fakers for real Black men/No more sliding by and hiding and riding/The fence/Take a stand, be a real man/Wage war on this non-sense!/

Man the fuck up! Not Man down!/As in "Down Low"/ Stop acting like a little Homo/Soldier!/Stop being a "Light Weight"/Rejoin the "Heavy Weights"/Or I'm gonna' send you to Judge Joe Brown's "Man Up" school/Rule/101/is check yo' hard headed ass son/This is man talk/Bullshit walks/

You say "Stop! We hear!" "What you dissing us for?"/You're just "sissies"/ you won't listen/stop that ass switching/More hard core/

I'm eliminating pranksters/I'm a "real" rap gangster/With a "Contract"/" To kill" weak raps/I'll make you a deal you can't refuse/Choose/to stop committing rap suicide, or prepare to lose/Your rap life/This ain't no hype/I know you hate me, I called you out/ You probably got rabies coming out your mouth/I know you gonna' come gunning/

but I ain't running/I "stand my ground"/
Unlike Trayvon, I'm firing the first round/

ok ET ("Extra Tom) you can use your
"Smart-Phone"/ to "phone home"/But on the
real, you're a fake crook/It's like your boy
"Nas" says, "Made you look"/Now put that
on Facebook/I see you ain't too gangsta' to
wear "The Cross"/If you lose yo' life, maybe
yo' soul won't be lost/ Like "The
Resurrection of Christ"/ I come to destroy
"The Thug Life"/I got no more time to waste/
DJ Long Arms, Base… I'M OUT OF HERE

STILL A SLAVE

I watched you and thought,
    "Still a slave"
As you down a pint of Jack Daniels (JD)
The bottle never leaving your mouth

And then the drama…

"Niggers better recognize, I ain't no punk"
From sun up to sun down drunk as a skunk

Down goes another pint,
not a drop do you waste
With that drunk ass Nigger grin
pasted on your face
"The White man's the devil",
you say, "He wants all us Niggers dead"
Down goes another pint,
liquid poison to the head

Then you pass it to Lil' Shorty, a "Forty"
He's only 12 years old
You say, "Drink this Lil' Nigga'
and be a man"
As this evil unfolds

You say the White man's the devil?
Then you must be his most trusted assistant

As you down another pint without any resistance

Jobless, homeless, useless, stupid and dumb
If I held the rope, this Nigger would be hung

I watched her and thought,
        "Still a slave"
As she says, "I played that Nigga.
See what he bought?"

And then the drama…

"You just like yo' damn no good ass Daddy",
You tell your little boy
"You ain't never gonna be no good"
"You lil' ghetto bastard"
"You never get out the 'hood"

"White mens are better than Niggaz"
You say, "I gonna' get me a white boy"
But White boys don't want no "Ghetto Ho"…
He'll use you like a toy
You're doing the White man's job
You're still a good Nigger winch
Breaking the Black boy down
From cradle to grave, inch by fuckin' inch

Heartless, selfish, spiritless,
rude and insane

If I had it my way
I'd put your dumb ass back in chains

I watched you and thought,
     "Still a slave"
As you stab another brother or sister in the back
Trying to advance on the corporate fast track

And then the drama…

"I'm the best African American for the job",
you say
This mental slavery pollutes your mind
 "Use me to keep these other Niggers in line",
you think
You're the" new" Nigger overseer.
Not worth a damn dime

Ruthless, clueless, insane in the brain
Call you "Mr. or Miss Toby",
proudly wearing your slave Masters' name

If I could, I'd put your silly Black ass back on
the auction block
Since you're already a "Sell Out", turning
back the clock

I watched them and thought,
     "Still a slave"

And then the drama…

Pants sagging, gun totting, dope slanging
Crime committing, gang banging
"Young Niggahz"
"My hommiez", "my 'hood", "do or die"
dumb Niggahz

The Chronic, wet ones, ya-yo, gin and juice,
always high – Niggahz
Bang- bang- rat- a- tat- tat- tat- Niggahz
Who you killing? - Niggahz

School- less, tool-less, foolish…Niggahz

If I had my way I would "Flip your Script"
And put all you "Young Niggahz" in line
with my homemade whip

I watched him and thought,
        "Still a slave"
Slamming "bones" on the prison yard
Bailing and mobbing with yo' 22 inch "guns"
A down ass "OG", still hard as hard
Inmate 243632…but to the "system",
just another "con"

And then the drama…

"These walls can't break me, I break them"
"White man can't break me, I break him"

So you do your bid,
because you're a third strike offender
But deep in your heart you know
you're a pretender

'Cause your little boy
is running wild in the streets
And within these prison walls is probably
where you two will meet
And just like back in the day, you kiss the
White man's dirty feet
'Cause that White man you talk about got
your dumb ass working for almost free

Yeah the White man can't break you,
you're already broke
Working on His "new" Plantation,
your prison cell is the "new" slave boat

I watched them and thought
        "Still a slave"
When the riots pop off, you go into a rage

And then the drama…

"Fuck the police! As you riot in the street
Burning down everything, you're a wild beast!

"No justice no peace!"
Is your battle cry
Funny how it was "just-us"
After the smoke clears who die
Just our neighborhoods burned to the ground
And just our dumb asses who burned our shit down

As long as you're still slaves…
We'll never be free

THE 'NIGGA' EXPERIMENT
(choose the group that you identify with)

Group 1

You actually love to call each other "Niggaz"
To you it's neither right or wrong
A term of endearment or a term of disgust?
Nigga Nigga Nigga Nigga, all day long

Hypothesis;

Words consciously and unconsciously
dictate actions
Actions are dictated by stimulus
Words have root meaning and expectations
The human mind's Power is limitless

The Laboratory

For the first day…
You can't say the word "Nigga"
After that, for the next day…
You can't even "think" the word Nigga
Lastly, for the last day…
You can't hear the word Nigga

Ready, Set, Go…

The Results – Did you do it? (yes/no)
Write below for each day.

Day 1_______________________________________

Day 2_______________________________________

Day 3_______________________________________

Conclusion; Were you affected (explain below)

____

____

____

Group 2

You never say or think the word "Nigger, Nigga"
You believe it's offensive and disgusting,
worse than a curse
You would never be caught calling another
person Nigger, Nigga
You'd rather be dead in a Hearse first

Hypothesis;

Words consciously and unconsciously
dictate actions

Actions are dictated by stimulus
Words have root meaning and expectations
The human mind's Power is limitless

For the first day…
Say the word Nigga Nigga , all day long
For the next day…
Read as many things you can find with the
word Nigga in it. In your books and songs
For the last day "think" the word till yo' mind
is gone

Oh yeah
For these three days, you can only use
Nigga in a "good" way

The Results – Did you do it? (yes/no)
Write below for each day.

Day1 __________________________________
Day 2________________________________
Day 3 _________________________________

Conclusion; Were you affected (explain
below)

Group 3

You use the word as a weapon, a dagger
It's a "killing" word, and you use it like that
"Punk ass Niggaz", "Bitch ass Niggaz"
"Nigga Killa"; by gun, knife, or baseball bat

Hypothesis;

Words consciously and unconsciously
dictate actions
Actions are dictated by stimulus
Words have root meaning and expectations
The human mind's Power is limitless

The Laboratory

For the first days…
You can only use "Nigga" to mean good
For the next days…
Write down all the times you heard the word
used in a good way "my Nigga', my Nigga'
For the last day think "Nigga is my friend"…

The Results – Did you do it? (yes/no)
Write below for each day.

Day1_________________________________
Day 2_________________________________
Day 3_________________________________

Conclusion; Were you affected (explain below)

____

____

____

The conscious mind is a puppet
When the stimulus says "jump"
it says "how high"
Now your unconscious mind has the
"Power of God Almighty"
With just a single thought you can choose to
"Live or Die"

"With just one thought …you could change
your world"

How many of you tried?
How many of you tried and failed?
How many of you didn't try at all?
Because for you, you like this "mind-made" hell?

Cultivate goodness in your self,
and goodness will be genuine.
Cultivate it in your family,
and goodness will flourish.
Cultivate it in your community,
and goodness will grow and multiply.
Cultivate it in your country,
and goodness will be abundant.
Cultivate it in the world,
and goodness will be everywhere.
-The I Ching -

TO LIVE AND DIE IN BLACK AMERICA
(A Swan Song)

Breathe…I can…Breathe…
What is this...?Air…
Light…I…See…Life
Pain…I…Feel…Pain…I Feel
Sound…I Hear…Noise…Fear…
I Sense…Fear…
Warmth…I Feel…Mother
Move…I Can…Walk…Cry…
I… Can…Talk…
Life…I Am…Alive…

Red, White, and Blue
This is the color of the dream of America
White, Black, Brown and everything in-
between
These are the colors of the people of America
Green (Money green)
This is the color of success in America
I am Black…
You say why is this important in America?
Greed…
Because of greed in America
Life…

This is the story of Black life in America

Broken down apartments, filthy streets, flies,
so many flies
That's the first thing I remember
Hoping, crying, scrapping for the 25th of
December
Rats, roaches, bed bugs, these are my brothers
Freezing cold, cramped-up toes
Us sleeping one on top of the other
Food scarce
Father left

Said he couldn't get a job
I asked him why. And not to lie
He said, "Whitey wants me to die"
Being a young one and still a dumb one
I wasn't quite sure what he meant
Looking tired. Looking old. I watched him as
he went

This is the next thing I remember…

Schools crowded. Teacher different
(I didn't know what White was yet)
Nose running, stomach feels funny,

hands are soaking wet
Classroom scary, but clean
Children fun, but mean
Ragged clothes; shoes too old;
can see my toes
Teacher looked (You know, in that funny way)
Some children laughed,
The few who had new clothes that day
I didn't understand
We all seemed the same to me
Why did they laugh? What did they see?
No one ever told me

I was poor

Mother working…Mother working…
Mother working
She seemed never to rest
Always scrapping, always scrapping
Always giving her best

This is life in Black America…

Ice cold winters, blazing hot summers,
Basketball, baseball, football
That's how you get out of the slums

What about hardball?
That's the White man's game
But I want to learn how to play too

Hanging out in the streets
I remember this next
Gang-bang, con game, dope selling, partying
with the freaks
And this is supposed to be my manhood test?

Shoplifting, stealing cars,
not thinking about a real job
Growing up wasn't easy to do.
In fact, it was damn hard

Women on dope. Men without hope
I think I've had enough

College…
A white collar job.
It couldn't be all that tough

Why do I have to study so long?
Something's wrong

And the next thing I remembered

was like being
Locked in prison
The educated ones call it
"Institutionalized Racism"

Suddenly I could see
(and I thought of my pops - my dad)
"Whitey's trying to kill me"

I could give up. Most of us had
What difference would one more make?
But like I said, I had enough
If they won't give, then I'll have to take!

Graduation...

I remember next
A day I will never forget
Mother proud. Family proud. Culture proud
But I haven't made it yet

LAW...
White man's justice. Black man's grief
No matter how educated, they treat me like a thief
Law and Justice. Just a bunch of jive
For Black folk it's the law of the streets

And only the strong shall survive

I remember homeboys dying young
At the hands of the White man's gun
I remember being arrested for being
In the wrong place
I remember saying I'm innocent,
The law slapped me in my Black face
You may think, He's overreacting
(if you're White)
These things are no longer true
But this wasn't 1948, this was 2002

Smothering oppression, capitalist obsession
These terms I learned later on
Red, White, and Blue. The American Dream
I'm an American, so why am I wronged?

I want to go home
To Afrika, "The Mother Land"
The origin of my heritage
My true birthplace
But I'm an African American now.
And American is my race

Overt. Covert. Intelligence

We know who's pulling all those strings
Being an educated Black, hardly means a thing

I won't cry. I'll always try.
I won't die. I'll multiply

This is life in Black America…

Bent backs. Face cracked. But pride intact
This is the legacy of the old ones before us
Helping hands. Making friends
Have you so soon forgot?
Respect your brother. Love your mother
This little means a lot
The past is a lesson soon forgotten
A luxury we can't afford
Let us be to each other like the old ones were
Let us make them proud of what they
sacrificed for

Blood lines. Extended family. Family ties
Let's go back to our roots
Genocide…
Am I paranoid? Or maybe it's the truth

Breath…Short…Air hurt…No…Breath…

Fuzzy…Eyes burn…Am I…Blind...?
Pain…I feel…Pain…All over…
What...You say something?... I can't hear…
Move…I can't…Move…Rigor Mortis,
I think…
Cry…I feel like…I…Won't…Cry…
Peace…I sense…Peace…
God…I sense…Love…
Death…I…Am…Dead

This is death in Black America
But the legacy must continue on…with you

AFERICA (A'fe'ri'ca)
(A New Movement)

This is an invitation to Rise Up!
Within America, Aferica has risen!
You are now the Master of your fate
Be you Black Muslim or Black Christian

Aferica is the power of Black people
within America
The power that all other ethnic groups already
know exist
The power to control who you are
by uniting as one people
The power that lifts you from the bottom,
to the top of the list

We Blacks in Aferica are the **16th** largest
economy in the world
Our spending power controls
"America, The Great"
And "He who controls America
controls the world"
"Money talks. Bullshit walks" …
On this there is no debate

Black money is the secret power that we
Black people have
And nobody else can come close to our power
The whole world fears and respects the power
of Black money
Rise Up! Our time is now. This is our hour!

The truth is, we're all we got
We have more American "ways"
than African "ways"
Although our African roots run deep
We're one hundred per cent "American made"

Imagine the power of forty million strong…
Speaking with one loud voice,
marching in one earth shattering step
Having one mighty right arm,
one mighty right hand
If one of us falls, you got thirty nine million,
nine hundred ninety nine to help

Imagine an army so strong…
The "million man" army of North Korea
would shake in their boots
And bow down to the power of Aferica

Because our trillions of dollars are more
powerful than any number of troops

Imagine an army so strong…
The Chinese would worship at our feet
Africa runs America, "the tail wags the dog"
A Lion isn't a Lion, if it doesn't have teeth

"The Secret"…
Do you want to know if the Illuminati is real?
 Contact me…
And the next steps will be revealed

blackilluminati333@hotmail.com

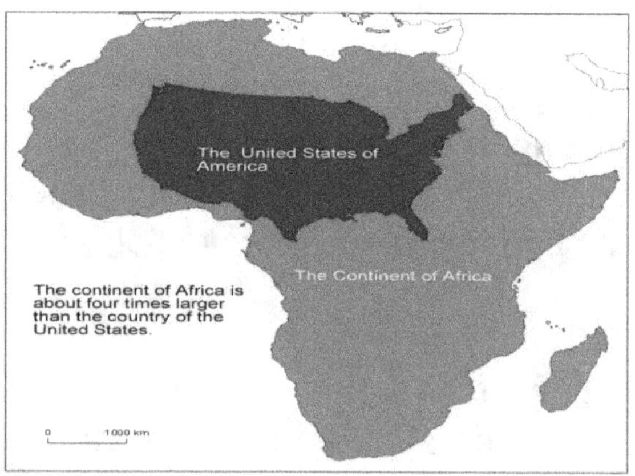

AND WHEN HE HAD OPENED THE
FOURTH SEAL
I HEARD THE VOICE OF THE FOURTH
BEAST SAY.
"COME AND SEE..."

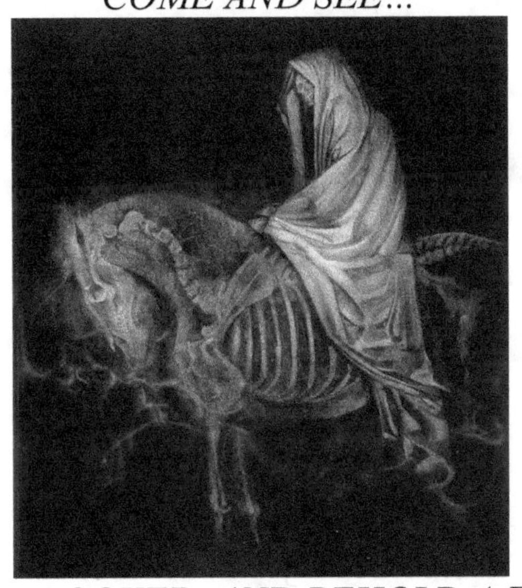

AND I LOOKED, AND BEHOLD A PALE
HORSE
AND HIS NAME THAT SAT ON HIM WAS
DEATH.
AND HELL FOLLOWED WITH HIM.

REV. 6:7&8

www.ingramcontent.com/pod-product-compliance
Lightning Source LLC
Chambersburg PA
CBHW051747250726
48659CB00001B/282